# MASTER THE NIC®:
# WRITTEN
# WORKBOOK

## Shonna M. Magee

Printed in the United States of America


ISBN  978-0-615-30437-3


Published by Shonna Magee LLC

## Shonna Magee LLC

Congratulations on taking a step towards passing your written exam! It doesn't matter if you are taking the national exam or a state exam. The information contained in this workbook will help you build a strong foundation of knowledge about interpreting. If you do not already have books related to interpreting, it is strongly recommended that you get those to use in conjunction with this workbook. This workbook has activities and questions whereas the books on the recommended reading lists for national and state exams have explanations.

If you have been to my **Master the NIC®: Written** workshop, you have heard me talk about **NOT READING** and you are already up to speed on why there are no answers in this book. If you have not been to one of these workshops, allow me to explain.

It makes sense that we will retain more information when we are engaged in a more active learning activity than a passive one. I had to think of how I could actively engage you, the "non-reader", in a workbook. If you simply read the answers, you will not retain as much as if you have to go seek out the answers and talk about them with colleagues. In order to get the answers to the questions in this workbook, you will need to find them in your reading materials, online, and through discussions with colleagues. This process will transform you from a passive learner into an active learner.

**How to use this workbook:** Be sure to complete the workbook yourself. Do not copy the answers from someone else's book because that is passive learning. Team up with a friend who is also studying for the written. Have a friendly competition with your study partner. Think of it like a scavenger hunt of sorts. Write notes, vocabulary words, etc on the blank pages. When you're done, exchange workbooks and correct each other's. Teach the material contained in this workbook to someone else. It could be your study partner, another colleague, or even a friend who doesn't know anything about interpreting but wants to help you study. If you do all of these things, you will retain more than you ever thought you could in a short period of time.

How do I know this works? I've helped many interpreters pass written exams with this method. Does this sound familiar? You start to read one of your text books, a minute or two goes by, your mind wanders, you start thinking about your lunch meeting you have tomorrow, your sister's haircut, if you turned the coffee pot off, then you have to go back and re-read. I like to call reading a form of self-hypnosis. It is a passive activity. If you stop reading and shift to a more active learning mindset, like reading with intent to teach or searching out answers, you will retain more information and be ready to take on any test! Good luck and be sure to visit us on the web for workshops, DVDs and other professional development resources. www.shonnamagee.com

Warmly,

# Workbook Table of Contents

### Check off each section as it is completed

**ACRONYMS- Write out the full name for each acronym.**

1. RID

2. NAD

3. MCE

4. SEE

5. AVLIC

6. AGBAD

7. NIC

8. CDI

9. CI

10. CT

11. OTC

12. SC:L

13. MCSC

14. CSC

15. IC

16. TC

17. QA

18. EIPA

19. EdITOR

20. DOE

21. LSQ

22. IDEA

23. ADA

24. ASL

25. LRE

26. IEP

27. SHHH

28. ITP

29. IEP

30. SSS

31. CASE

32. CEU

33. VRS

34. TRS

35. VRI

36. FCC

37. LTA

38. NTID

39. PSE

40. LOVE

41. CPC

42. CODA

43. HVO

44. HLAA

45. DPN

46. SSP

47. WASLI

48. WFD

49. SPP

50. NMM

**ACRONYM WORD SEARCH- Find the complete spelling of each of the acronyms in the puzzle below.**

```
U Q Z Y S C X D J O T F C T G H P R M H
Y V B A Y F O W Y N U R R A E E R D L X
S M E R F M X S J U J I N K F P O I N G
N I M D C M Z R J H R L O I P O T J F N
F F O C Q L A Z I P Y E K I O D A Y H I
Y N F O Q N O S E O Z N D L D G R O Q T
I J E M U O L T N Y Y N P J P L T X U E
W X S T V I I I O Q A O L P I G S G U R
E O H H F T T N C X U S B M D Y I U E P
V T W R A A P U I C H R K I G G N J Z R
C K R E L T G N A C O E G S I U I S J E
X W E P Q N T O V L J P X I N Y M H N T
M S T E I E V I P M T T I G S P D E P N
Q S E T Y I V T C W Y R R N I P A B U I
B K R E H R I A C Z W O T S G L T N E T
A N P T Q O D C F S B P S U N R S V G O
T M R I U L E U J S E P R P E H E P U M
C E E V T A O D M R F U N P D O T Q Z M
O U T E X U R E J E J S X O E T L Y L E
H J N S V S E G D K N D L R N U A P K R
Y K I T S I L N B R A E J T G T C P H O
W K F R D V A I Y A L T D E L V O D X E
Z K A A P H Y U X M P H Z D I K L F P D
I U E I K G S N C L N G J S S Q L S A I
S E D N Y I E I Q A O I P P H G N X D V
M N D I Y H R T G U I S F E J O U C Q M
A O E N O C V N S N T T K E W O A J R U
F Z I J W R I O A A A Y K C X J M C T Z
G I F U Y Y C C Z M C J M H H T E R W H
K Z I R A V E J G N U M V E J A R D S I
C L T Y A N R O U O D Q C E B M I H M J
J U R Z L G V X J N E P Z F M X C S B L
V J E F B P J Q M F L G N Z M X A I R Q
Z A C B Q H E Y H X A T I Y D T N L P S
U Q D P K G K S U T U P G Q W X S G S X
T U P U C B V W R E D J Z C N O I N J D
H N R M U V Y Q H A I Q P H M E G E D R
A P Q C K B S Y E L V B G M R F N D Y F
J C B T E P F U F D I J M K Z Y L E T E
R U K K U F G T R A D D S U P U A D W L
F A O U B I H P E O N H E S A M N O V Q
F P C Q O C K P Y K I Q Z C Z C G C M P
B L X Y Z R F F C D B V N A R N U Y Z K
I A R H G Y N F V X X C H Y P B A L H Q
O J F I W B G R Q B U S I M X W G L A L
P M F D U B A Q E B X I P Y E V E A Q T
S O U M O J J I X K T P W Q Y S R U F C
Z A T S K B I S J A I Y O Q R C L N Y W
R J E X Q Y O X Q Q T X D J T B Z A H L
A V H N W F Q V D E G N N O W K R M L X
```

| CDI | CEU | HVO | IEP | MCE | NMM |
|-----|-----|-----|-----|-----|-----|
| PSE | RSI | SSS | VRS | VRI | LTA |
| ASL | SSP | RSI |     |     |     |

**VOCABULARY- Define and discuss each of the following terms. Can you teach someone else what they mean? Can you explain the following terms to someone who is not affiliated with interpreting?**

1)      Interpretation

2)      Transliteration

3)      Translation

4)      Processing Time

5)      Voice-to-Sign

6)      Sign-to-Voice

7)      Source Language


8)      Target Language

        .


9)      Tactile Interpreting


10)     Oral Transliteration


11)     Teaming


12)     Dynamic Equivalence


13)     Clozure Skills

14)     Consecutive Interpreting

15)     Simultaneous Interpreting

16)     Cultural Mediation

17)     Chunking

18)     Glossing

19)     Total Communication

20)     SimCom

21) Language

22) Loan Signs

23) Lexical Borrowing

24) Affect

25) Fingerspelling

26) Classifiers

27) Register

28)   Non-Manual Markers

29)   Contact Varieties

30)   Mouth Morphemes

31)   Grammar

32)   Morphology

33)   Syntax

34)   Phraseology

35) Phonology


36) Pragmatics


37) Semantics


38) Prosody


39) Discourse Analysis


40) Phoneme


41) Morpheme

42)     Free Morphemes

43)     Bound Morphemes

44)     Topic-Comment Structure

45)     Sign Supported Speech

46)     Conceptually Accurate Signed English

47)     Code Switching

48)     Rochester Method

49)    Inclusion

50)    Discourse Mapping

**WHO'S WHO: Write a brief explanation of the following individuals.**

1. Thomas Hopkins Gallaudet

2. Laurent Clerc

3. Abbe Charles-Michel de l'Epee

4. Juliette Gordon Low

5. I. King Jordan

6. Laura C. Redden Searing

7. Julius Wiggins

8. William Elsworth "Dummy" Hoy

9. Alice Cogswell

10. Andrew Foster

**WHICH IS WHICH?** Write an **L** next to the communication methods that are languages. Write **RL** next to those that are representations of a language.

_____ PSE                 _____ SEE1                 _____ Spanish

_____ ASL                 _____ CASE                 _____ SEE2

_____ English             _____ MCE                  _____ LOVE

_____ SE                  _____ Cued Speech          _____ Rochester Method

**LONG ANSWER-** After reading each question, choose a position and defend it with resources, references, etc. When you are done, defend the opposite position.

1. Should interpreters tutor at the K-12 level?

2. Should hearing people be allowed to teach ASL?

3. Are CODAs better skilled interpreters?

4. Should interpreters attend Deaf events regularly?

5. Should all working interpreters be nationally certified?

**OPEN QUESTIONS- Answer the following with as much detail as possible. Discuss your answers with at least two colleagues.**

1. What is AUDISM?

2. What does "reciprocity of perspectives" in oppression mean?

3. Give me an example of "horizontal hostility" in oppression.

4. Who was the first deaf president of Gallaudet?

5. What liberation movement helped see him into the president's office?

6. What are the main tenets of the Code of Professional Conduct?

7. What is "vicarious trauma?"

8. Explain the HELPER interpreter philosophy is no longer recommended for the profession.

9. Explain the MACHINE/CONDUIT interpreter philosophy and how it can be ineffective.

10. Explain the BI-BI interpreter philosophy and why it is the model most followed today.

11. What does "linguistic expansion" mean?

12. What does "cultural expansion" mean?

13. What does "cultural/linguistic reduction" mean?

14. Are cultural/linguistic expansions/reductions ethical as interpreters?

15. It takes twice as long to make a sign than speak a word but communicating in ASL takes the same time as English. Why?

16. Give an example of contrasting for "I'm tired."

17. Give an example of noun listing for "country."

18. Give an example of couching/nesting for "bed."

19. List 3 reasons that professions have code of ethics.

20. When was RID established?

21. Where was RID established?

22. Give four examples of External Noise.

23. Give four examples of Physiological Noise.

24. Give four examples of Psychological Noise.

25. Give two examples of Equivocal Language.

26. Give four examples of Euphemistic Language.

27. Give two examples of an abstract word.

28. Give four examples of Passive Voice.

29. Give two examples of a HEDGE.

30. Give two examples of a HESITATION.

31. Give two examples of an INTENSIFIER.

32. Give an example of a POLITE FORM.

33. Give two examples of a TAG QUESTION.

34. Give two examples of a DISCLAIMER.

35. Give two examples of FROZEN REGISTER.

36. Give two examples of FORMAL REGISTER.

37. Give two examples of CONSULTATIVE REGISTER.

38. Give two examples of INFORMAL/CASUAL REGISTER.

39. Give two examples of INTIMATE REGISTER.

40. Explain Linguistic vs. Paralinguistic features of language.

41. What is appropriate attire for interpreters?

42. Name three ways to get a deaf person's attention.

43. What is "Deaf Time?"

44. What percent of deaf children are born to hearing parents?

45. _____% of the world is of a collectivist culture.

46. _____% of the world is of an individualist culture.

47. Mild hearing loss is a _____dB loss to a _____dB loss.

48. Profound hearing loss is a _____dB loss to a _____dB loss.

49. Moderate hearing loss is a _____dB loss to a _____dB loss.

50. Severe hearing loss is a _____dB loss to a _____dB loss.

51. What is the Rochester Method?

52. Give an example of SEE1.

53. Give an example of SEE2.

54. What is does CASE mean?

55. What does PSE mean?

56. What does MLS mean?

57. Interpreting for a deaf-blind person is called _____ interpreting.

58. What additional information does an interpreter give while interpreting for a deaf-blind person?

59. The term "Speech Banana" means what?

60. What is the difference between decibels and frequency?

61. What is the difference between interpreting and transliterating?

62. What is the difference between deaf and Deaf?

63. What is the difference between SEE1 and SEE2?

64. What is the difference between L1, L2 and L3?

65. What is the difference between interpreting and translating?

66. What is the abuse reporting hotline for your state?

67. What are reciprocal signals?

68. What are three resources for improving your interpreting?

69. List five elements of culture.

70. Explain three similarities between spoken and signed languages.

71. Explain three differences between spoken and signed languages.

72. How might an interpreter prepare him/herself for difficult subjects that are unfamiliar?

73. How does the ADA define a "qualified" interpreter?

74. Explain each of the elements of the ADA's definition of a "qualified" interpreter.

75. Under the ADA, which part of the definition of "qualified" is lacking if you interpret for your family?

76. Under the ADA, which part of the definition of "qualified" is lacking if you are asked to omit information?

77. Under the ADA, which part of the definition of "qualified" is lacking if you don't understand the terminology at an assignment?

78. Under the ADA, which part of the definition of "qualified" is lacking if you sign in English to a deaf person who uses ASL?

79. Explain what a conflict of interest is. Give five examples.

80. How might a staff educational interpreter have differing roles than a freelance interpreter?

81. In a medical setting, how might the administration of certain medications affect the interpreting process?

82. What does "equal access" mean to you?

83. What does "empowerment" mean to you?

84. How might a CODA or SODA have cultural pressures as interpreters?

85. Name five ways in which you could show your support for fellow interpreters.

86. Why should interpreters examine how they normally speak when they are not interpreting?

87. Name two skills that an interpreter would need that are unique to theatrical interpreting.

88. Name two skills that an interpreter would need that are unique to legal interpreting.

89. Name two skills that an interpreter would need that are unique to educational interpreting.

90. Name two skills that an interpreter would need that are unique to medical.

91. Describe five differences between a staff interpreter and a freelance interpreter.

92. What is the difference between VRS and VRI? Who pays for each?

93. What word is not spelled in the Rochester Method?

94. Why should an interpreter be aware of light sources in an interpreting setting?

95. Name three ways you can help prevent or slow the progression of Repetitive Motion Injury.

96. In what cases might a Certified Deaf Interpreter be needed?

97. How might passive voice create difficulties for an interpreter?

98. How might abstract words create difficulties for an interpreter?

99. Explain the Topic-Comment grammar structure.

100. What are the differences between simultaneous and consecutive interpreting?

101. List pros and cons to being a staff interpreter.

102. List pros and cons to being a freelance interpreter.

103. Explain how characterization can clarify a message.

104. List 5 questions you would ask an interpreting agency before becoming a staff interpreter with them.

105. List 5 questions you would ask an interpreting agency before becoming a freelance interpreter with them.

106. List 5 questions you would ask an interpreting agency before accepting an assignment.

107. What are your state licensure laws (if any) related to interpreting?

108. How might the role of a K-12 educational interpreter change depending on the grade of the student?

109. What type of information could an interpreter share at an IEP meeting?

110. Name three ways in which a K-12 interpreter might empower the student.

111. Describe the evolution of the interpreting profession.

112. Name three things that team interpreters should discuss before working together on an assignment.

113. How does process time differ with interpreting vs. transliterating?

114. How do mouth movements differ with interpreting vs. transliterating?

115. How does signing space differ with interpreting vs. transliterating?

116. Explain why an interpreter and deaf consumer might invent signs and what cultural rules apply.

117. Explain three reasons why an interpreter should show up early to an assignment.

118. What are some cultural values to Deaf people?

119. What are some cultural traditions of Deaf people?

120. Identify and discuss three events televised nation-wide that were associated with deaf people.

121. What are the duties of Vocational Rehabilitation? How they can be a resource for deaf individuals?

122. What are the duties of Deaf Service Centers? How can they be a resource for deaf individuals?

123. Discuss the different types of assisted listening technologies available to deaf individuals.

124. What does an accessible environment look like?

125. Why might interpreters need handouts or materials that are to be discussed during an assignment?

126. What is the philosophy of inclusion?

127. Discuss support for inclusion.

128. Discuss support for schools for the deaf.

129. Discuss support for raising a child with a Cochlear Implant.

130. Discuss support for raising a child with an English-based signing system.

131. Discuss support for raising a child with ASL in the Deaf Community.

132. What are the different causes of deafness?

133. Explain how we hear.

134. What is the difference between decibels and frequency?

135. What would you include in your interpreting contract with regards to "no shows"?

136. What would you include in your interpreting contract with regards to a minimum number of hours?

137. What would you include in your interpreting contract with regards to travel charges/considerations?

138. What would you include in your interpreting contract with regards to cancellations?

139. What would you include in your interpreting contract with regards to the need for team interpreters?

140. What would you include in your interpreting contract with regards to breaks and billing for breaks?

141. Show three examples of indexing in ASL.

142. How might initialized signs differ in ASL than in an English-based signing system?

143. How to prepositions differ in ASL than in an English-based signing system?

144. Explain the facial expression for WH questions in ASL.

145. Explain the facial expression for yes/no questions in ASL.

146. Describe symptoms of Carpel Tunnel Syndrome.

147. How does confidentiality differ among interpreting settings? (Educational, college, medical, legal)

148. Explain why being an interpreter/aide could pose difficulties.

149. Explain why being an interpreter/tutor could pose difficulties.

150. How might you deal with a hearing consumer who is unwilling to deal with interpreters?

151. Why is the term "hearing impaired" considered culturally unacceptable?

152. Name 4 ways to get a deaf person's attention.

153. What is Cued Speech?

154. Why might a person who is clinically hard-of-hearing label him/herself as deaf?

155. Why might a person who is clinically deaf label him/herself as hard-of-hearing?

156. If an Oral Deaf person is trained to lip read, why might s/he still need an oral transliterator?

157. The term "minimal language skills" is now referred to as what?

158. What is the difference between CASE and SEE1&SEE2?

159. How might the issue of time differ among cultures?

160. How might the issue of spirituality differ among cultures?

161. How might the issue of family differ among cultures?

162. How might decision-making differ among cultures?

163. What is a person's schema?

164. How does oppression affect the minority?

165. How does oppression affect the majority?

166. How might knowing the effects of oppression affect you, the interpreter?

167. How might the interpreter oppress a deaf or hearing consumer?

168. How should interpreters feel about deaf people making jokes about hearing people?

169. How might the oppression of deaf people affect the interpreter?

170. Are interpreters experts on Deaf Culture?

171. What are initiation jokes played on hearing people who are new to ASL and the Deaf Community?

172. What is sight translation?

173. What is the difference between interpreting and translating?

174. What are content elements of English?

175. What are the functional elements of English?

176. Give 5 examples of directional verbs.

177. What is Usher's Syndrome? What are the different types?

178. What is Waardenburg Syndrome?

179. Discuss three instances where an interpreter would need to culturally mediate.

180. Besides testing, name three ways in which an interpreter can be evaluated.

181. Why would public speaking skills be important for interpreters?

182. Discuss why it is important for an interpreter to maintain a low profile.

183. Should an interpreter voice in first person or third person?

184. How many hours per week on average should an interpreter work before burn-out?

185. Describe the difference between general liability insurance and professional liability insurance.

186. Describe the difference between professional liability insurance and errors/omissions insurance.

187. How does HIPAA affect the interpreter?

188. When interpreting for a deaf-blind consumer, what other attire considerations should be made?

189. How long can an interpreter work alone in a low-stress assignment before needing a team?

190. How long can an interpreter work alone in a high-stress assignment before needing a team?

191. Describe how a team of interpreters can effectively switch.

192. What is subject-verb agreement?

193. What are noun-verb pairs?

194. Who was Alexander Graham Bell and what was his contribution to the deaf?

195. When is Deaf History month?

196. What could cause an interpreter to lose his/her certification?

197. What are regional signs and how can they affect interpreting services?

198. What are home signs and how can they affect interpreting services?

199. How does a cochlear implant function?

200. How might Video Remote Interpreting affect community interpreters?

# LINGUISTIC MATCH-UP

Directions: Match the definition to the term

1. _____ Morpheme

2. _____ Phoneme

3. _____ Bound Morpheme

4. _____ Morphology

5. _____ Semantics

6. _____ Pragmatics

7. _____ Lexicon

8. _____ Prosody

9. _____ Pronominalize

10. _____ Discourse

a. a grammatical unit that never occurs by itself, but is always attached to another morpheme

b. the total inventory of morphemes in a given language

c. the smallest unit in the sound system of a language

d. The study of patterns of word formation in a particular language, including inflection, derivation and composition

e. to replace a noun or noun phrase with a pronoun

f. communication of thought by words; talk; conversation longer than a sentence

g. the smallest meaningful unit in the grammar of a language

h. the stress and intonation patterns of an utterance

i. the analysis of language in terms of the situational context within which utterances are made, including the knowledge and beliefs of the speaker and the relation between speaker and listener

j. the meaning, or the interpretation of the meaning, of a word, sign, sentence, etc.

# CROSSWORD

**Across:**

1. A commencement speech made by a university president to the audience is an example of _____ register.
4. The National Anthem is an example of _____ register.
7. "She's so pretty, isn't she?" is an example of a _____ in powerless speech.
8. A philosophy in which the interpreter is too rigid, cold, and takes no responsibility for the communication.
10. "Umm, uh, er" are examples of _____ in powerless speech.
13. A philosophy in which the interpreter mediates between two languages and two cultures.

**Down:**

2. "This may be just my opinion, but...." is an example of a _____ in powerless speech.
3. A register that includes a teacher giving a lesson, a lawyer giving advice and a doctor giving medical information are all examples of the _____ register.
5. "If you don't mind and if it's not too much trouble...." is an example of a _____ in powerless speech.
6. "You know...sort of...kind of..." are examples of _____ in powerless speech.
9. A conversation between neighbors would fall into the _____ register.
11. A philosophy in which the interpreter is very rigid but is aware of placement and lighting is the _____ facilitation.
12. "It really is such an unbelievably amazing honor..." is an example of _____ in powerless speech.
14. A philosophy in which the interpreter is too involved and sometimes makes decisions for the deaf person.
15. A conversation between spouses or siblings is considered in the _____ register.

MULTIPLE CHOICE: Answer the following multiple choice questions. Make note of any unfamiliar vocabulary terms in this section and write them on the "Additional Terms to Study" page immediately after this section.

1. Which of the following is the most accurate form of interpreting?

    a. Simultaneous

    b. Transliterating

    c. Referencing

    d. Consecutive

2. Which law has provisions for a "free and appropriate education"?

    a. Rehab Act of 1973

    b. Article Act 151

    c. P.L. 94-142

    d. ADA of 1990

3. What percentage of deaf children are born to hearing parents?

    a. 80

    b. 60

    c. 100

    d. 90

4. How much of new programming is required by law to be captioned?

    a. 80%

    b. 90%

    c. 95%

    d. all new programming

**5. Which law provided children the right to placement in the "least restrictive environment" or LRE?**

    a. P.L. 99-457

    b. Rehab Act of 1973

    c. the ADA of 1990

    d. P.L. 94-142

**6. Each of the following is important to discuss with your team before team interpreting except:**

    a. how to give the other a feed

    b. technical vocabulary related to the assignment

    c. hourly pay

    d. length of interpreting time before switching

**7. Which law provided the right for an Individual Education Plan or IEP?**

    a. P.L. 94-142

    b. P.L. 99-371

    c. The Rehab Act of 1973

    d. the ADA of 1990

**8. In an IEP meeting, interpreters would be able to provide information about all of the following EXCEPT:**

    a. the student's ability to participate and interact with others in the classroom

    b. student's comprehension of instructional vocabulary and concepts

    c. the student's attention span

    d. the student's grades in classes

**9. The ADA was enacted and signed into law in which year?**

    a. 1990

    b. 1980

    c. 1973

    d. 1999

**10. P.L. 94-142- The Education for All Handicapped Children Act of 1975 was amended and renamed:**

    a. The Americans with Disabilities Act

    b. The Children with Disabilities Education Act

    c. The National Ability of 1742 Act of America, Inc.

    d. Individuals with Disabilities Education Act

**11. As an educational interpreter, you are expected to do all the following EXCEPT:**

    a. make the room accessible

    b. explain what the teacher is saying if the student becomes confused

    c. make the source language into an equal message in the target language

    d. communicate non-verbal information to the teacher

**12. Classroom teachers can assist in communication by:**

    a. asking the interpreter to clarify any misunderstandings the student has

    b. asking the interpreter to interpret only educational material presented in class

    c. asking the interpreter to move from the front of the class

    d. involving the student in activities and talking directly to him/her

**13. Which of the following is not needed to prepare to interpret in a college class?**

    a. an overview of the week's lesson plans

    b. to know if the student is prepared and has done his/her homework

    c. a list of technical vocabulary related to the lesson

    d. a copy of the class text

**14. A subject area teacher should:**

    a. introduce the interpreter to the class at the beginning of the semester, attend related in-service workshops and direct questions to the interpreter to make sure the deaf students are understanding

    b. provide an overview of upcoming instruction, seat the interpreter and deaf student in a place that will least disrupt the class, and notify the interpreter in advance of planned media presentations

    c. include all students in class activities, encourage students to participate in answering questions, and be responsible for any problems that occur in the classroom

    d. introduce the interpreter to the class at the beginning of the semester, ask the interpreter to explain any confusions, let the interpreter set up the positioning

**15. The main responsibility of the interpreter in the classroom is to:**

    a. help the students understand the material presented

    b. facilitate communication

    c. tutor the students

    d. help the students with their English

**16. The changes made to P.L. 94-142 under the Individuals with Disabilities Education Act (IDEA) include all of the following EXCEPT:**

    a. Children are referred to as "disabled" rather than "handicapped"

b. The title of the law was changed from The Education for All Handicapped Children Act

c. States are required to provide services to private schools as well as public

d. Services are extended to include deaf-blind children

**17. Which was the landmark law that guaranteed civil rights for all disabled people?**

a. Rehab Act of 1973

b. P.L. 94-142

c. Americans with Disabilities Act

d. IDEA

**18. In what year was the RID established?**

a. 1964

b. 1972

c. 1968

d. 1961

**19. The language from which an interpretation is based is called:**

a. Target Language

b. Source Language

c. Initial Language

d. Operative Language

**20. Meaning is derived mostly from:**

a. Intonation

b. Actual words

c. Body Language

d. Equivocal Language

## 21. Code-switching happens when:

a. interpreters have the ability to interpret in different codes

b. interpreters identify and match the language preference of the deaf consumer

c. Deaf people in a conversation change from ASL to a more English-based signing mode when hearing people become involved in the conversation

d. interpreters work with a client who is fluent in both ASL and Signed English and must continually switch back and forth depending on consumer preferences

## 22. Translation is:

a. the same as interpreting

b. the same as transliteration

c. the same as interpreting but with a written component

d. the same as interpreting but with a video component

## 23. All of the following should be a part of your contractual agreement EXCEPT:

a. a 2-hour minimum

b. portal-to-portal or mileage

c. cancellation policy

d. meal reimbursement

## 24. Another name for "lag time" is:

a. processing time

b. delay time

c. lead time

d. translation time

**25. AFFECT means:**

a. consequences of ethical decisions

b. facial expression and intonation

c. mood of participants in the interpreting situation

d. internal dialog of the interpreter

**26. AUDISM means:**

a. the aural abilities of deaf consumers

b. the study of hearing

c. discrimination based on hearing status

d. a hearing disorder

**27. An example of physiological noise is:**

a. you being hungry

b. someone in the room coughing

c. random thoughts that pop in your head

d. a light in the room flickering

**28. Euphemistic language is used to:**

a. deliver a message with the most sophisticated vocabulary possible

b. deliver a message in a more direct or blunt manner

c. deliver a message without intonation or facial expression

d. deliver a message in a softer, more delicate manner

29. **The ADA of 1990 defines a "qualified interpreter as one who has all of the following    EXCEPT:**

a. impartiality

c. specialized vocabulary

b. certification

d. accuracy

30. **Which of the following is an example of PASSIVE VOICE?**

a. I hope it's not too much trouble.

b. The lamp was broken.

c. I don't mind whatever you'd like to do.

d. It's raining cats and dogs.

31. **Which of the following is an example of EXTERNAL NOISE?**

a. a light flickering in the room

b. you feel faint

c. random thoughts and judgments

d. any noise you can't hear

32. **When you experience the pain of your consumers, this is called:**

a. suffering by proxy

b. traumatic proxy

c. vicarious experience

d. vicarious trauma

**33.** Saying something specifically so that it can be understood in two different ways is called speaking in:

   a. linguistic mediation

   b. euphemistic language

   c. equivocal language

   d. expansion


**34.** Introductions in the Deaf world may include all of the following except:

   a. asking how old one is

   b. asking if one's parents are deaf

   c. asking where one went to residential school for the deaf

   d. asking if one knows certain people from the same area


**35.** While platform interpreting, one should:

   a. make sure everyone watches the interpreter

   b. sign larger than normal and keep fingerspelling to a minimum

   c. stand in the center of the stage where all the action is

   d. sign smaller to avoid distracting the hearing people


**36.** Which of the following is the most culturally sensitive and acceptable term:

   a. Deaf-Mute

   b. Hearing-Impaired

   c. Hearing loss

   d. Deaf/Hard-of-Hearing

**37. A person's frame of reference or background experiences is also called a person's:**

    a. schema

    b. expansion

    c. semantic

    d. affect

**38. Clarifying a concept by means of giving examples or contrasting is also called:**

    a. expansion

    b. construction

    c. back translation

    d. identification

**39. An example of an ABSTRACT word is:**

    a. midnight

    b. weapon

    c. quiet

    d. yellow

**40. Which of the following contains a TAG QUESTION?**

    a. Is this a good color on me?

    b. She's a good singer, isn't she?

    c. Really? I can go to the reception?

    d. How many dogs are there?

**41. Which of the following shows judgment?**

    a. "I" statements

    b. "It" statements

    c. "But" statements

    d. "You" statements

**42. The National Anthem is an example of which linguistic register?**

    a. Frozen

    b. Consultative

    c. Formal

    d. Intimate

**43. Interpreting at a doctor's appointment is interpreting which linguistic register?**

    a. Frozen

    b. Consultative

    c. Formal

    d. Intimate

**44. Of the world's cultures, \_\_\_\_% are collectivist and \_\_\_\_% are individualist.**

    a. 30, 70

    b. 50, 50

    c. 70, 30

    d. 10, 90

**45. Which one of these includes the other three?**

    a. CASE

    b. SEE

    c. Rochester Method

    d. MCE

**46. Which type of interpreting should be done in courtroom settings?**

    a. Consecutive

    b. Linear

    c. Abstract

    d. Simultaneous

**47. Who was Laurent Clerc's educational interpreter?**

    a. I. King Jordan

    b. Lou Fant

    c. Charles L'Eppe

    d. Thomas Hopkins Gallaudet

**48. PL 94-142 made the biggest impact on deaf education by:**

    a. requiring mainstreaming for all deaf students

    b. requiring the opening of more deaf residential schools

    c. preventing public schools from denying enrollment of deaf students

    d. requiring deaf students to be educated by deaf teachers

**49. The Rehab Act of '73 impacted which group of people the most?**

    a. College students

    b. Preschool children

    c. Elementary school students

    d. Middle and High School students

**50. Interpreters working in high-stress environments are likely to suffer from:**

    a. Carpel Tunnel

    b. Repetitive Motion Injury

    c. Mental burnout

    d. All of the above

**51. What should interpreters do to help an assignment run smoothly:**

    a. meet with the consumers to determine language preferences

    b. receive materials ahead of time to prepare for unfamiliar or technical vocabulary

    c. brief consumers who have never worked with an interpreter before

    d. All of the above

**52. Which of the following registers includes someone with "expert" status?**

    a. Consultative

    b. Intimate

    c. Frozen

    d. Formal

**53. Which of the following is a sign parameter?**

a. affect

b. eye gaze

c. handshape

d. classifiers

**54. Which of the following is the same in both interpreting and transliterating?**

a. mouth morphemes

b. using conceptual signs

c. length of processing time

d. grammar structure

**55. Which of the following is not a provision under the ADA?**

a. Deaf people have the right to a certified interpreter

b. auxiliary aids and services must be provided to deaf individuals unless it causes an undue burden

c. Doctors may not bill deaf patients for interpreting services

d. Employers may not discriminate against deaf individuals in hiring for a job

**56. During an interpreting assignment, if the deaf person gets angry and curses at the hearing consumer, the interpreter should:**

a. choose a more appropriate word for that environment so the hearing person isn't offended

b. interpret the message the way the deaf individual intended

c. inform the deaf person that it is inappropriate

d. inform the hearing consumer that the deaf person cursed but do not say the actual word

**57. The Rehab Act of '73 applies to:**

a. private colleges

b. private and public colleges

c. public colleges that receive federal funding

d. all Vocational Rehab students

**58. Which of the following provides the least amount of information on the language preference and fluency of a deaf consumer?**

a. If the deaf consumer comes from deaf or hearing parents

b. If the deaf consumer was educated in a deaf school or a mainstreamed public school

c. If the deaf consumer uses hearing aids or other assisted listening devices

d. If the deaf consumer is actively involved in the Deaf Community

**59. All of the following is true about noun-verb pairs except:**

a. the noun is indicated by a smaller, double movement

b. the verb is indicated by one movement

c. they use the same handshape

d. nothing, the context indicates if it is the noun or the verb

**60. When an interpreter is asked to give testimony as an expert witness, s/he is most qualified to discuss:**

a. deaf education

b. linguistic and cultural mediation

c. Deaf Culture

d. psychological aspects of deafness

# ADDITIONAL TERMS TO STUDY

**FILL IN THE BULLETS:** Write in all the information you know about each law.

**Rehabilitation Act of 1973 (as amended by Public Law (P.L.) 99-506 and P.L. 100-630)**

- 
- 
- 
- 
- 

**Public Law 94-142 The Education for All Handicapped Children Act of 1975**

- 
- 
- 
- 
- 

**P.L. 101-476- Education of the Handicapped Act Amendments of 1990**

- 
- 
- 
- 
- 

**The American's With Disabilities Act of 1990 (ADA)**

- 
- 
- 
- 

**Telecommunications Reform Act of 1996**

- 
- 

**Child Protective Laws**

- Phone number:_____
-

**STICKY SITUATIONS- How would you handle these sticky situations? Which tenets in the Code of Professional Conduct would you reference? Which laws apply?**

1. While interpreting in a very rowdy high school classroom, the general education teacher asks you to only interpret the educational material and leave out the disruption so that your student's education is not compromised.

2. You are an interpreter in a mental health facility with a deaf client you've worked with on several occasions. You know that this individual has severe emotional and anger outbursts that can get quite violent. Today, your usual team is out and you have a team who has never worked with this client before.

3. In a mainstreamed class, the teacher tries to move your seat closer to the door every day. You explain that you have seated yourself in a position that assists in the best visual access to you, the teacher and the visual material presented. The teacher still insists on moving your seat every day.

4. You interpret at a long-term assignment at a university under an agency. You are working with a team and both of you are freelance interpreters with several agencies. Both of you have heard that the university is looking for cheaper interpreters. The next week you happen to see your team interpreter's business card on the deaf student's desk. You ask the student where she got the business card and she says that your team gave it to her to give to the university since that agency has cheaper interpreters.

5. You are substitute interpreting in a college class. You've introduced yourself to the client and answered all of his questions before the class started. While you are interpreting, the deaf client tries to chat with you during the lecture.

6. You are hired to interpret a meeting for employees of a company. When you arrive, you are introduced to the 2 deaf clients. One is an oral deaf person and the other uses only ASL. You ask if there's another interpreter coming and they tell you that you are the only one interpreting today.

7. You are interpreting a Better Business Bureau luncheon for a deaf man who is a CEO of his company and trying to network with other businesses in the city. Everyone gets their lunch and sits down for a presentation from the BBB representative. While you are interpreting, you notice that the deaf man is chewing very loudly. It is starting to attract the attention of the other guests at the luncheon.

8. You are interpreting a diabetes counseling appointment where the counselor is instructing the deaf woman on an eating plan to regulate her blood sugar. She proceeds to tell the deaf woman that there are no carbs in tomatoes or carrots. You know that this is not true.

9. You are sitting in an IEP meeting as a member of the team. An ESE specialist recommends that the deaf student take after-school tutoring classes but states that the student doesn't need an interpreter.

10. You work for a VRS company with about 20 other interpreters, many of whom are from the same place of worship. It has come to your attention that one of the interpreters is reporting other interpreters to the elders at his place of worship for associating with interpreters who are gay. Now there seems to be a lot of tension in the air at the call center.

11. An interpreter in your school district never comes to the workshops, pre-planning meetings, or even the post-planning meetings that the school requires of all interpreters.

12. A deaf student asks you to interpret a phone call for her. You suggest that she use the school TTY or VP. She tells you that there isn't a TTY or a VP at the school. You know that there are plenty of payphones for the hearing students but the deaf students do not have a way to place personal calls.

13. You are asked to substitute for an interpreter for 2 weeks. Upon arriving at the school you meet the very seasoned interpreter you will be working with. She is wearing red nail polish, a ring on every finger, and about 5 bracelets.

14. You interpret for a deaf student whose mother is employed at the same school. One day the mother asks you how her daughter is doing. You know that the child got a 98 on a really hard math test and has also received a P.E. award for her athletic ability.

15. You are a non-CODA interpreter working with an interpreter who is a CODA. After several instances of working with her, you equate her ethical decision-making skills as non-existent! You have tried to approach her on this and she implies that she has so much influence in the Deaf Community that no one would ever dare to report her for fear of being black-balled in the community.

16. You work at a college campus with a few other interpreters. One day, one of your colleagues tells you that one of the deaf students was requesting that you not interpret one of the classes anymore. You're not sure if it's the deaf student who wants to get rid of you, or the interpreter!

17. You have expressed your concern to another interpreter about some of her behaviors that you feel do not coincide with the code of professional conduct. This causes some tension between you and the other interpreter. She has many years of experience and you are fairly new to the profession.

18. You notice that a male interpreter at your school is being very friendly and flirtatious with the female deaf students. He has even gone so far as to help his deaf student with a class project and has done almost the entire assignment.

19. While in a classroom, you overhear the other site interpreter mention that she has been having correspondence with a student's mother about certain materials that the student needs to bring in. She states that it is not a big concern since she is only letting the mother know what materials are needed.

20. Upon starting at a new school, you find out from your students that the other interpreter on campus is bad-mouthing you to them. The other interpreter has been at that same campus for many years and this is your first year there. You're sure she's badmouthing you to the staff as well.

68 | P a g e

© Shonna Magee, 2009
Reproduction of this workbook, in whole or in part, is strictly prohibited

21. You are interpreting at a Social Security appointment for a deaf woman. She has brought along her son who is about 4 years old. During the appointment, you notice the little boy playing with a truck on the floor. You also notice that he has what appears to be cigarette burn marks on his legs.

22. Your student is absent and you end up subbing for a sick interpreter at another school. Upon arrival, the classroom teacher attempts to have small talk with you by asking you everything about what you do at your regular school, including the names of the students you interpret for.

23. Your school district has a policy or practice in place that states that all interpreters will sign in English to any deaf student. You are working with a student whose communication preference is ASL.

24. While visiting your agency one day, you notice that there is a planner on the lobby coffee table. You look in it to find out who it belongs to and see that it belongs to one of the interpreters who works there. The planner also has information on the interpreter's assignments for the last 2 weeks.

25. You are scheduled to interpret for an all day assignment starting at 8am. You managed to negotiate a really good rate for this job so you're looking forward to going. That same morning, you wake up with allergy problems so bad you can barely breathe. You know that if you take allergy medication, it will make you somewhat sleepy.

26. You are hired by the circuit court to interpret for a deaf man who is going to court ordered AA meetings. The circuit court is requesting that the interpreters report back to them if the deaf man shows up for the meetings or not.

27. You are working for a VRS company as an independent contractor. One day your manager calls in to the service and gets you as her interpreter. She asks that you connect to a phone number in her office. She says she will pick up the phone and set it on the desk so the minutes will rack up because your call center will make more money if there are more billable minutes. You know that the economy is tight and jobs are being cut.

28. You are called to interpret in an outpatient mental health setting with a patient you've never met before. When you arrive, you introduce yourself to the patient. Both of you are called back to an office where a nurse asks some basic information questions. After she is finished she says that she needs to make copies and that the two of you can stay in the room until she comes back.

29. You are called to interpret for a commencement ceremony. You arrive and are greeted by the coordinator who places you in a very appropriate position to interpret on the right side of the stage. It allows for access of deaf consumers without being a distraction to anyone else. During the commencement ceremony, a videographer tells you he needs you to move to the left so he can film a certain segment. He's insisting that you move and interrupting you as you work.

30. You are interpreting for a committee meeting, where the members are trying to develop a policy on hiring interpreters. Afterward, they ask you information about the interpreting profession, about your agency and others, and about policies and fees for interpreting services.

31. You are interpreting for a four-day workshop. After the first day, the Deaf consumer asks to have lunch with you and your teammate as he is the only Deaf person and cannot communicate with the other parties.

32. Assume you are a certified interpreter and you are interpreting for a legal deposition, which is expected to take several days. On the first day, the Deaf person asks to have lunch with you and your team interpreter.

33. You are interpreting at a college full time. One day while you are on break relaxing in your car, one of the hearing students in the classroom opens your passenger door and sits in your car. You wonder what he is doing there when you see him pull out a bag of marijuana.

34. One day while interpreting at a medical school, the professor is discussing the various layers a needle has to go through in order to do a lumbar puncture. When the next layer of discussion is fat, he stands behind you and says, "the next layer is something she has more of than me." You are mortified when the students answer, "fat!"

35. You are working with an interpreter teaming on-site at a conference. The interpreter is from that area but you drove in for this assignment. When your team is "on" she signs many words differently. She's a certified interpreter so you try to give her the benefit of the doubt but some of what she is signing makes no sense.

36. You are an interpreter recently hired on at an agency. The agency has a study group for interpreters wanting to take the national certification exam. You decide to attend the study group. While you are there, one of the interpreters hands you a study packet. In the study packet there is a paper that matches the state exam exactly! You just took your state exam last week so you know this comes directly from the test! The study packets are going around to all of the interpreters.

37. You are interpreting in a college setting for a deaf woman returning to school after being an at-home mom for many years. Ever since the first day she has tried to cling to you, even during your break time, for security.

38. You are interpreting between a boss and a deaf employee. The boss is chastising the employee for being late and starts to get quite rude. For some reason, the employee thinks that the comments are coming from you, the interpreter, and starts to direct his comments back to you.

39. You are called to interpret at a doctor's office. When you begin to interpret, the doctor tells you not to sign because the deaf person can read his lips. The deaf person signs, "I don't understand" but the doctor insists that she can read his lips and tells you to stop every time you lift your hands.

40. You are interpreting in a mainstream classroom for a deaf student. In the middle of the first day, it is apparent that all of the students are watching you sign. The teacher tells at the class to stop watching the interpreter and to pay attention to her. The deaf student raises her hand and says, "but I have to watch the interpreter."

41. You are working at a local high school for a deaf student. The office calls you down because the student was just busted for smoking marijuana in the bathroom. The school has called the police and they are all expecting you to interpret.

42. You are interpreting in a college classroom with a deaf student who rarely pays attention to you. Most of the time she has her nose in her Sidekick. When she bombs the mid-term exam, the teacher asks her what happened. She responds with, "My interpreter didn't interpret all of the information to me."

43. You are interpreting at a personal fitness class on a university campus. The instructor of the class tells you that you cannot be in the gym without sneakers on. The problem is that you interpret a business class immediately before and a marketing class immediately after this class. There's no way you can change your business attire.

44. Before an interpreting assignment, you meet up with your team to get ready, discuss logistics, etc. While the two of you are talking, you notice the smell of liquor on your team's breath and start to notice indications that your team is drunk.

45. You are having coffee with a deaf friend and she begins to tell you about a horrible experience she recently had with an interpreter that you realize you know very well. She tells you many nasty details and basically insinuates that the interpreter was useless and unprofessional.

46. You are an educational interpreter for a deaf student whose hearing parents are being investigated by Child Protective Services. Every time CPS has gone to the home, they fail to bring an interpreter and rely on the parents to interpret what the child is saying to the case worker. You know that the parents don't sign but the CPS worker doesn't know that.

47. You are interpreting for a client who is about to buy a house. They haven't hired a realtor and the realtor who represents the seller tells them that they don't need one. You just bought a house and know how much your realtor did for you. You don't want the deaf client to get ripped off.

48. You are in a waiting room at a doctor's office. The deaf consumer is there and starts chatting with you about how she had to stop her medication 3 weeks ago because she couldn't afford it. When the doctor calls you both in, he asks the deaf woman if she's been taking her medication. She replies with, "yes."

49. You are an interpreter for two deaf kids going to a crafts class in the community. One day while interpreting, the two deaf kids start bickering back and forth saying things like, "stop touching me" and, "you kicked me first!"

50. You are interpreting a VRS call and in the middle of the call the deaf consumer threatens to call your boss. He says that you have a horrible attitude when you are interpreting. You know that your attitude is part of the interpretation because the hearing person is being very snotty.

51. You've interpreted for a client who has a bad habit of making sexual remarks towards female interpreters. Your friend was just hired at the same agency and has an appointment at the same location you've been to while interpreting for this specific client. You want to make sure she is prepared for what is going to happen.

52. You are interpreting at a conference for a very educated deaf attendee. During the course of one of the small breakout sessions, the deaf man asks a question in the middle of the presentation. He signs and you voice politely, "Excuse me, I have a question…." and then continue to interpret the deaf man's question. The presenter answers the question and then follows by saying, "And please do not let him interrupt again."

53. You know an interpreting student who is trying to get intern hours. One day when you are going in to interpret in a college class, you see her chatting with the deaf student. When they see you, the interpreting intern states that she met the deaf person at Deaf Club and asked if it was ok to observe the class. The deaf person agreed but the interpreting student never asked you to intern under you.

54. You are good friends with an interpreter in your area. You know she has been volunteering her time, making phone calls for the Republican Party for the upcoming election.

55. You are called to substitute for an interpreter at a regular appointment for three weeks in a row. When you show up for the third week, the hearing client runs into you in the parking lot and says, "I'm so glad when I see you show up. The other interpreter who is normally here is horrible. She has her own conversations with the deaf people, doesn't interpret everything, dresses inappropriately and talks continuously about her love life."

56. Your agency calls you to interpret at a college medical class at a school you've never been to before. When class is about to start, the teacher asks if there are prayer requests. The deaf student sees that you are confused and informs you that this is a private and religious school. Your agency never informed you of this because if they had, you would have passed it onto another interpreter since you don't share the same religious views as the school.

57. You are interpreting for an Anatomy and Physiology class at a local university. During this course, students will be required to enter the cadaver lab. There are rules regarding anyone who enters the cadaver lab that they must wear a lab coat. Lab coats are white which definitely does not contrast with your skin tone.

58. You are interpreting at a job interview. When the person conducting the interview turns around, the deaf client steals something off her desk.

59. You are an educational interpreter and your 12-year-old deaf consumer tells you that she might be pregnant and needs your help.

60. You work for a company that requires certification to interpret. One night while on the RID website, you search for your colleagues' names to see if their test results are posted. You want to send congratulations cards. You discover that one of your co-workers isn't even a member of RID so she can't possibly be certified.

61. You and your team are working a week-long orientation for new hires. You agree to switch every 20 minutes. When you switch her, she says she needs to use the restroom and doesn't come back for 20 minutes. This happens every time you are interpreting.

62. A good friend of yours is also an interpreter. She has marriage counseling with her deaf husband and has asked that you interpret for their sessions. She says she only trusts you to interpret well and to keep your mouth shut about her personal business. She doesn't trust any of the other local interpreters to keep her business confidential.

63. You are interpreting a training about sexual harassment. In the middle of this training, the speaker goes off on a tangent about something work related. Everyone else in the room seems to understand what he is talking about but you have no idea. You felt qualified to interpret for this training but now he's speaking about something else entirely.

64. You are interpreting for a woman who is in labor. During her waiting process, the nurse tells you she is going to check on another patient and she wants you to make sure the deaf woman's contractions are timed.

65. You are called to interpret for a client who is receiving free legal services through Legal Aid, a non-profit service. They are requesting that you provide pro bono services as well.

66. You are scheduled to interpret with a team for an all-day assignment. Your team comes in amped on 4 energy drinks, coffee and ginseng tablets because she stayed up all night.

67. You are working with a team interpreter and realize when she is in the hot seat that she is chewing gum.

68. You are interpreting for a deaf woman who is making a phone call. During the phone call, you realize that she is giving her bank account number and social security number to someone who is telling her that she's won the African lottery.

69. You are interpreting a presentation that is using a slide show. All the lights in the room are off except the one that is being used to illuminate you. Unfortunately, that light starts flickering.

70. You are interpreting in a college classroom with a team interpreter. You are in the hot seat and when it comes time to switch, you look over and find your team interpreter sleeping on the desk.

71. You are attending a seminar on Deaf Education for which there are interpreters for the deaf participants. One of the interpreters can barely sign. You understand the deaf participants just fine but the interpreter can't seem to voice for them at all!

72. You are a certified interpreter and your CEU cycle is almost up. You are 2 hours shy of completion but don't see another opportunity to earn CEUs except your friend's workshop. The problem is that her workshop is on the same day as your sister's wedding. Your friend has offered to add your name to the list of attendees.

73. You work for a VRS company as a video interpreter. One day you are verbally abused by a deaf caller. You decide that you should not interpret for this person in the future so you communicate this with your managers. They tell you that you must answer the call because all calls must be answered within the shortest time possible to be in compliance with FCC regulations. You try to explain that the caller was abusive towards you but your managers still insist that you answer that person's calls.

74. You are an interpreter aiming at national certification but are not there yet. While working for a VRS company, there are several legal phone calls. You try to switch out of these calls with an interpreter who is qualified to interpret legal settings but your management has a policy that requires you to interpret those calls.

75. You are called to interpret for a deaf consumer you have interpreted for numerous times before. You know that this person has gone to three different emergency rooms for pain killers because you've interpreted for all three. Now she is in the fourth emergency room complaining of severe back pain.